To my beloved son, whose unwavering love sustains me through life's challenges, guided by our creator. A̲s̲t̲, we embrace grace and persist̲e̲

My deepest gratitude I extend to family and friends. Your encouragement and unwavering support have made this therapeutic book for our children possible.

And to all young dreamers and creators, may these pages be a canvas for your imagination as you journey through them—a wellspring of peace, joy, and boundless inspiration.

"The only way to do great work is to love what you do." — Steve Jobs

**Special thanks to our dear friend "Lo" (Lenora) for her relentless encouragement.*

Made in the USA
Monee, IL
06 January 2025